The Bike-Owner's Handbook

by Peter Drinkell
with a foreword by Graeme Fife

Contents

Foreword

I cycled to Timbuktu once. Don't ask. Someone had to. There were three of us and the youngest member of the party, a dab-hand at all things teckernickerlogical, found me on the morning of our departure fumbling with my front brake. It was malfunctioning as, indeed, on this occasion, was I. He levelled at me that look which is both pitying and contemptuous and said: 'Why don't you do what you're good at – go and pay the bill.'

Now, there are two levels of mechanical expertise, the basic and the all-embracing. I managed, though who can possibly say how, to claw my way up from complete incompetence to the basic level and there I have stayed. It's true, I did once remove the engine of an old Rover, take it to pieces, get the crankshaft re-engineered and put the whole thing back together again (it started first time). However, that was with the close aid of a workshop manual backed up by that most precious of advantages, bravado overlaid with sheer ignorance. Besides, there is, somehow, more to disturb the hapless amateur about a bicycle. It's more, well…finicky.

Ball-bearings were my downfall. I had the temerity more times than was advisable to undo bottom brackets in the days when they came with spindles, races, lock-nuts and (I shudder) ball-bearings. Easy to liberate but, like car keys, small children and New Year resolutions, endowed with an instinctive tendency to go missing. I remember too well the bile of exasperated fury rising in my gorge to break out in terrible frustration at my doomed efforts to reassemble the wretched gubbins, the bearings as resolutely elusive as beads of quicksilver. Dear reader, do not go there. That way madness lies.

This said, the fact is you don't know you're born, these days. You have cassettes, plug-in and do-up sealed units from which no moving part can escape. No matter that component manufacturers are still bent on flummoxing the chancy amateur with all manner of other tricks of finickiness which are essential to the bicycle's existence, the absence of ball bearings is a boon for which you should be unfailingly grateful.

Nevertheless, there are areas of mechanical competence approachable by even the basic level novice. It really does behove you to explore and master them. I am not talking anything more complicated than changing tyres, inner tubes and brake blocks. On these items your safety most assuredly does depend. I record with some dismay another dosage of the withering look as I replaced a dodgy tyre under the scrutiny of a mechano-freak. 'I've thrown away better tyres than that' he said, with undisguised scorn. I was not immune. I blushed and took the point, even if not immediately.

It is, therefore, with the zeal of a convert to regular maintenance of the beautiful machine that I welcome this book. It does the business, the essential business. Help and guidance where most emphatically needed. For my own part, I would add this counsel, given to me by a good friend whom I had asked to check out a fairly new transmission which was sticking. 'Nothing wrong with it, only…' he paused, smiled wanly and added, in what I must describe as an embarrassed whisper, 'it's filthy.'

Clean your bike, keep it running smooth, free of shit and grit, nicely but not too lavishly oiled and not only will it treat you better but, no small consideration, every cleaning keeps wear at bay and is, thereby, money in the bank.

Graeme Fife
Sevenoaks

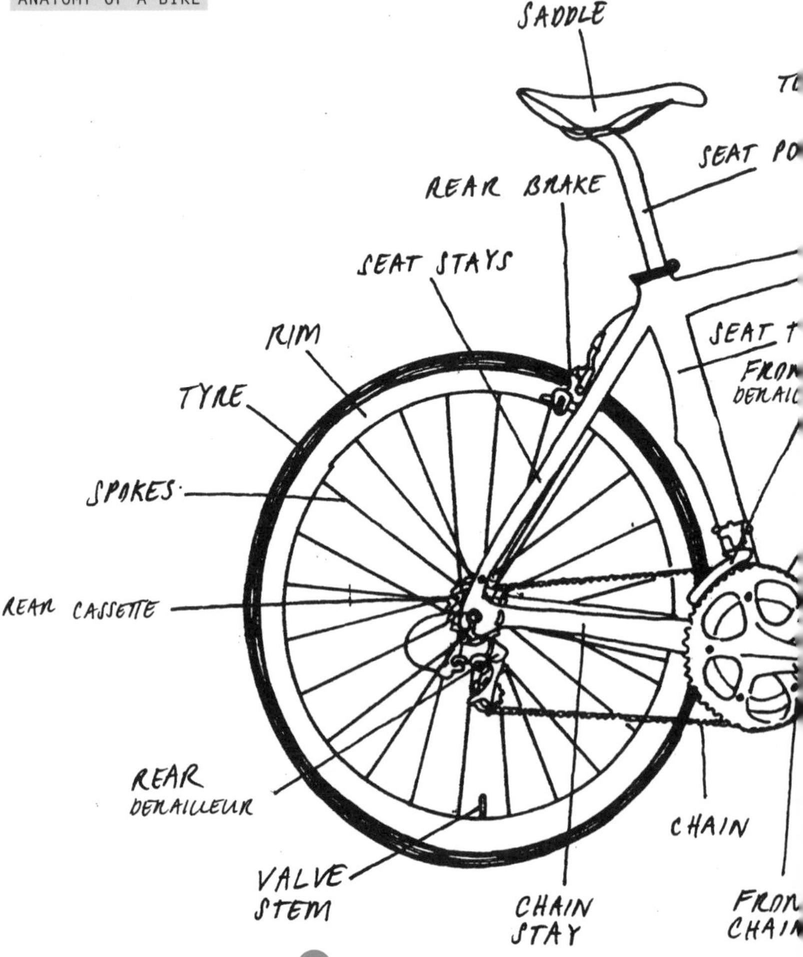

SADDLE

T(

SEAT PO

REAR BRAKE

SEAT STAYS

SEAT T

FRON
DERAIL

RIM

TYRE

SPOKES·

REAR CASSETTE

REAR
DERAILLEUR

CHAIN

VALVE
STEM

CHAIN
STAY

FRON
CHAI

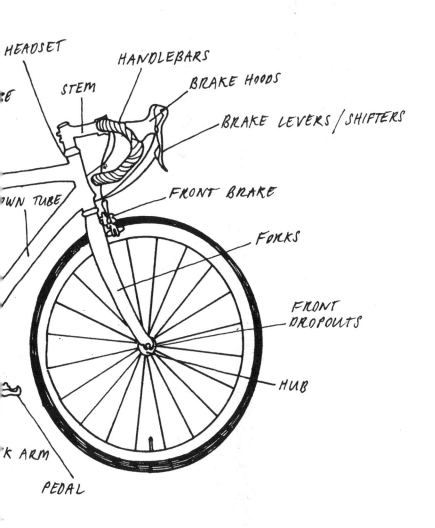

HEADSET

HANDLEBARS

STEM

BRAKE HOODS

BRAKE LEVERS / SHIFTERS

E

WN TUBE

FRONT BRAKE

FORKS

FRONT
DROPOUTS

HUB

K ARM

PEDAL

Puncture Repair

Punctures happen. It's a sad but inevitable part of cycling, and there's only one thing worse than riding along a deserted road at night and getting a flat, and that's riding along a deserted road at night in the rain and getting a flat. In wet weather your tyres are softer and stuff sticks to them easily. Stuff being bits of glass, shards of flint, sharp bits of twigs, and pretty much anything else. What I'm trying to say is that if there's one thing you need to know about your bike it's how to fix a puncture.

Fixing a puncture can seem fiddly and complicated to begin with, but once you've done it a few times it will come naturally. And the great thing about learning how to fix a puncture is that in doing so you'll get to know your bike. A bicycle is a wonderfully simple machine. But even in its simplicity it is made up of lots of components that rely on each other, that function in synchronicity to propel the machine forward. Once you get to know some of the basic components, the machine as a whole starts to make sense.

There are a few essential things that you'll need to carry with you at all times: A pump, a multi-tool (with a selection of Allen keys), an inner tube and a puncture repair kit. You might wonder why both an inner tube and a puncture repair kit are required. The answer is that the best way to fix a puncture is not to fix a puncture.

If you carry an inner tube around with you, you will save yourself the immense hassle of locating and mending a tiny hole in the middle of an inevitably inconvenient and probably quite wet location. The repair kit is for when you've fixed the tyre and 5km down the road you mysteriously pick up another puncture.

Which leads me to the primary rule of puncture repair. Check and check again to find out what caused your puncture, and get it the hell away from your tyre so that it doesn't get you again.

If you can spare a little time, practice puncture repair at home. Take your time with it, and get to know your bike in the process. Once you get in tune with your bike, it will change the way you cycle. You'll be able to listen to your bike and treat it with kindness – checking tyre pressure, brakes and chain regularly, keeping it running smoothly, and rewarding yourself with a much more enjoyable ride. You might also find yourself noting your environment a little bit more closely – keeping an eye out for glass or grit on the roads, carefully avoiding potholes and rocky surfaces. Because cycling is at it's best when you feel at one with your machine and the world around you. That's when everything truly works in synchronicity.

STEP 1: REMOVING THE WHEEL

When working on your bike it's always easiest to create a clean and stable platform to work on by turning it upside down. To do so safely, reach over the bike, taking hold of the seat stay and the fork, and flip it towards you.

Now you'll need to remove the offending wheel. The back wheel is a little trickier than the front, due to the rear cassettes, but in both cases, the first thing you'll need to do is to release the brakes so you can ease the wheel out. Most modern brakes have a quick release that lets the brake arms open up easily. If your brake does not have a quick release, you'll have to let some air out of the tyre to get it past the brake blocks (see pp. 22-23).

The three main brake quick release mechanisms:

V-BRAKE

PULL NOODLE TOWARDS YOU
AND PRESS THE BRAKE
ARM IN.

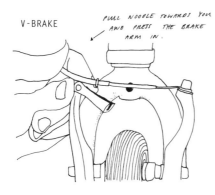

CAMPAGNOLO

PRESS BUTTON ON SHIFTER

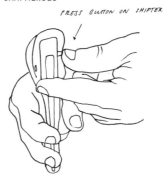

CALIPER

RELEASE

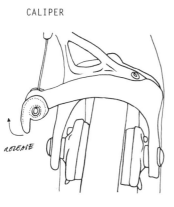

REMOVING THE FRONT WHEEL

After releasing the brake, simply undo your quick release levers or wheel nuts (see right) and guide the wheel out of the front fork away from the drop out. You may notice that there are little lips on the front drop outs. These are safety mechanisms known as 'lawyers lips', there to prevent your wheel falling off if your quick release becomes loose while riding. You may need to undo the quick release a little more to get it past the lips.

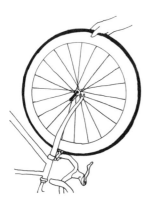

QUICK RELEASE

For the most part, modern bikes are fitted with a quick
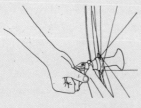 release skewer. Take the quick
release lever and pull it
away from the bike frame. This
unlocks it and should loosen
it enough for you to hold the
friction nut on the opposite
side and turn it a few times,
enabling you to release the
wheel. Don't undo it all the
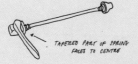 way - just a few rotations will
do the trick. If you do undo it
all the way, just rememeber -
the tapered end of the spring
should face to centre.

TAPERED PART OF SPRING
FACES TO CENTRE

WHEEL NUTS

If your bike is fitted with wheel nuts (as is the case with
 most fixed gear bikes), you will
need the appropriate sized
spanner to undo them, and must
carry this with you at all
times.

To take your back wheel off, you'll need to get past your chain and rear cassette, and to make this a little easier, the first thing you'll have to do is put your bike into its highest gear on the rear cassette and the lowest gear on the front chainring. This will create more slack in the chain, making it easier to pull the rear derailleur back, and also to slip the wheel back on later.

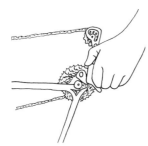

Undo your quick release levers or wheel nuts (as per p.17). Now stand behind your bike, take hold of the rear derailleur body and pull it towards you with one hand. This will free up the chain, allowing you space to release the wheel from the rear dropout with the other hand. Pull the wheel out at a slight angle, away from the derailleur body.

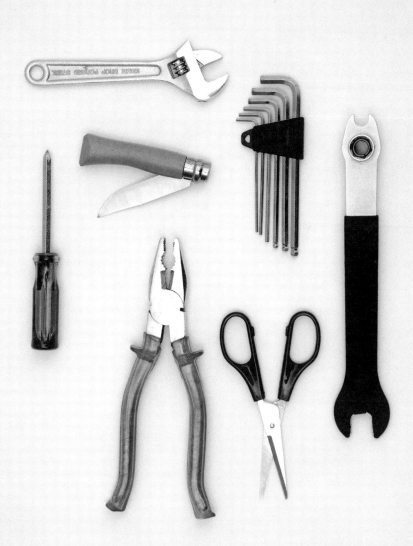

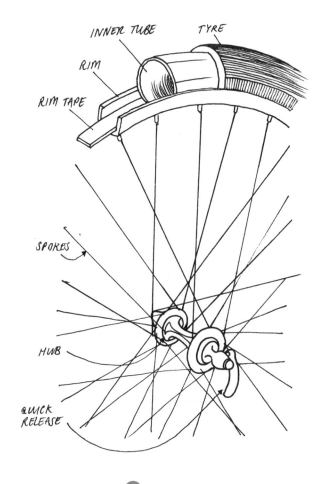

INNER TUBE

TYRE

RIM

RIM TAPE

SPOKES

HUB

QUICK RELEASE

PUMPS

Tyres lose air every day, and you need to check them every time you ride to make sure they are properly inflated. Look on the wall of your tyre. You should see two numbers followed by 'PSI'. This stands for pounds per square inch, and relates to the pressure rating of your tyre. Inflating to the lower number will make the ride more comfortable, inflating to the higher number will make your bike more efficient and puncture resistant.

A track pump is an essential bit of kit to have at home. It rests on the floor and gives you greater leverage to pull and push full strokes with the handle - great for high pressure tyres. They also have a pressure gauge so that you can inflate your tires to the correct PSI.

Portable pumps come in two types - frame fit pumps and mini pumps. This is the pump you will carry with you at all times. Look for a pump that is double action - filling on both the upstroke and the downstroke.

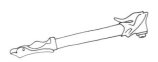

PRESTA VALVE

This type of valve is for high pressure, usually thinner tyres, and is commonly found on road bikes. For the most part you'll come across short (or standard) Presta valves, but occasionally more expensive road bikes with deep section rims will have a long Presta valve. The bike shop will be able to tell you which one you have.

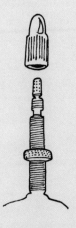

To release the air from a Presta valve, unscrew the nipple at the end of the valve. Then press the pin in towards the rim of the bike. If there is a nut at the base of the valve where it meets the rim, remove this. The dustcap and the nut do not need to go back on afterwards (the nut especially is not necessary).

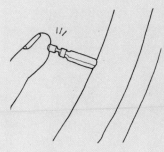

SCHRAEDER VALVE

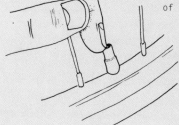

Schraeder valves are the fatter car-type of valve, and are mostly found on mountain and hybrid bikes. These tyres are heavier duty and run at a slightly lower pressure.

To release the air, remove the dustcap and use your nail to press in the pin at the centre of the valve.

STEP 2: EXTRACTING THE INNER TUBE

Now you've removed the wheel you'll need to extract your punctured inner tube using your tyre levers. Before you start this process, have a look at the wheel and see if you can see what's caused the puncture. Is there a bit of glass or stone still stuck in the wheel? Take a mental note of where this is in relation to the valve or mark the tyre with a pen, so that you can find the puncture on the inner tube once it's out.

Start by removing all the air from the inner tube. How you do this depends on what type of valve your bike has (see pp. 22-23).

Now you need to remove the tyre. Do this by pressing the tyre wall inwards, away from the rim. As you do so, you will see the hard edge at the base of the tyre begin to appear. This is called the bead.

Find a point roughly opposite the valve. Taking care not to

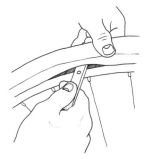

pinch the inner tube, insert your tyre lever under the bead of the tyre, securing the end onto a spoke. Now, on the same side of the tyre, carefully insert the second tyre lever two spokes along to the right, releasing some more bead. Then do the same two spokes to the left.

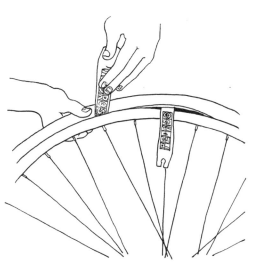

Now that you have a good section of bead unhooked, place

the tyre lever under the exposed bead at a flat angle to the rim and slide it all the way around, unhooking the rest of the bead. Make sure you don't run the tyre lever at right angles to the rim, or you'll risk tearing the inner tube.

With one side of the tyre released, you can now begin to extract the inner tube. Start opposite the valve and work your way around.

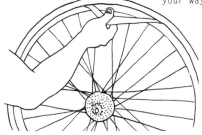

When you get to the valve, you'll need to get it out of the hole. On a larger tyre like a mountain bike, you may be able to simply press the valve out, but on a higher pressure tyre, you will need to peel the tyre back to be able to remove the valve.

Your inner tube is removed! Try to avoid placing it on the ground to prevent it collecting any debris that may cause even more punctures. If there's nowhere else to put it, hang it around your neck.

Now your inner tube is out, you have another opportunity to find the cause of your puncture. I keep harping on about this, but really I can't emphasise how important it is to find whatever caused your puncture so that it doesn't get you again.

Do this methodically. Pump up your inner tube to locate the hole and try to relate this back to the tyre. I would suggest taking the entire tyre off the rim so you can turn it inside out and inspect it thoroughly. At the very least, run your fingers along the inside of the tyre. Sometimes glass or sharp sticks can snap, leaving fragments on the inside.

While you're there, check the condition of your rim tape. This is the fabric or plastic tape that lines your wheel, protecting the inner tube from the spoke heads. It can become worn with age, allowing the spoke heads to rub on the inner tube. If punctures keep happening without obvious cause and your wheels are quite old, this could be an explanation.

Now you need to find the hole on the inner tube. It is easiest to do this at home, so if you have a spare inner tube with you, use this until you can search for the hole and repair it in a dry and well-lit environment.

Inflate the punctured inner tube and give it a once over to  see if you can locate the hole. If you can't, hold the inflated inner tube close to your upper lip and move it round. Can you feel the air escaping? If not, hold it close to your ear. Can you hear it?

If it's still not apparent and you are at home, you can submerge the inflated inner tube in sink of water and look for the stream of bubbles.

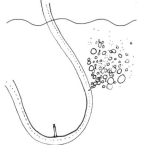

If you still can't find the puncture, the problem could be with your valve. Hold the valve in a cup of water, and look closely to see whether there are bubbles escaping. If there are you'll need a new inner tube.

Once you've found the puncture mark it with a pen.

STEP 4: FIXING THE PUNCTURE

Once you've located the hole and marked it, let all the air out of the inner tube.

Take the sandpaper supplied in your little kit, and roughen up an area around the hole slightly larger than the patch. Then wipe it clean. This creates a better bonding surface for the patch to adhere to.

Apply a thin layer of the vulcanising rubber solution, again covering a larger surface area than the patch. Let this dry for at least two minutes (or longer in cold weather). It needs to be dry/tacky for the patch to stick properly, so make sure you don't rush this.

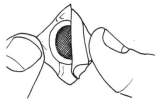

Take the patch out and peel off the protective layer (usually a piece of foil). Don't remove the transparent film at this stage and avoid touching the adhesive side of the patch – any oil or dirt on your fingers will stop the patch sticking properly.

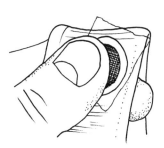

Now place the patch over the hole. Using your nail, work the patch from the centre outwards to get a good seal, ensuring there are no loose edges. Apply firm pressure to the patch and inner tube for at least a minute. If you do this by holding it between your palms, the heat will help the glue to bond.

Remove the transparent film from the patch by folding it

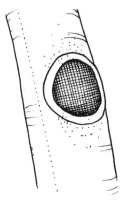

in half and peeling from the centre (not from the edge).

TIP: Some puncture repair kits come with a bit of chalk. If yours doesn't, it's worth carrying some with you. Once the patch is on, you can crumble the chalk or sprinkle some talc on it, creating a protective layer between it and the tyre wall.

Don't pump up the inner tube until it's inside the tyre; the pressure of the tyre wall will ensure a better seal on the patch.

STEP 5: REPLACING THE TYRE

If you have taken the whole tyre off, start by folding one side of it back onto the rim. This should be pretty easy.

Take your inner tube and inflate it slightly, so that it just starts to take shape. Don't put too much air in or it will be difficult to put the rest of the tyre on. Fit the valve through the valve-hole, making sure it's not in at an angle, and then work around, fitting the tube back into the tyre.

Once the tube is in, you can fit the other side of the tyre back onto the rim, starting at the valve. Once you get a third of the way along, go back to the valve and press it up to make sure that the seat, the bit around the shaft of the valve where it meets the inner tube, is up above the bead of the tyre. If it's below it, when you pump the tyre up, it will pop the bead out.

PUSH VALVE UP

Work the rest of the loose bead back onto the rim with your thumbs, alternating sides as you go around. This will get increasingly difficult as you near the end. Try to avoid using a tyre lever. This is usually possible with a little perseverance. If it's really stiff, go back around the rim massaging the tyre wall to help reseat the bead.

Now your tyre is back on, inflate the tube so that the tyre takes shape and then release the air. With the palms of your hands, massage the wall of the tyre, pushing the bead away from the rim all the way around on both sides. Occasionally the inner tube can get trapped or pinched under the bead. You should be able to pop it back under easily. If you don't, when you pump it up to full pressure it is likely to pop with an almighty bang.

TIP: When putting your tyre back on, try to make sure that the manufacturer's logo on the sidewall of the tyre sits over the valve. This will give you a reference point, so that next time you can match up the hole in the inner tube with the hole on the tyre.

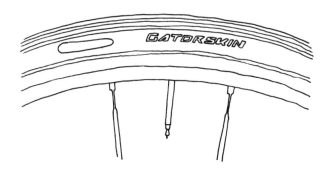

STEP 6: REPLACING THE WHEEL

You're really almost there now - you just need to put the wheel back on your bike and cycle off into the sunset.

FRONT WHEEL

With the bike upside down and the quick release levers undone, pass the wheel between the forks and guide the axle onto the front dropouts, making sure it is all the way in. Firmly tighten the quick release skewer so that you have to really apply force to close the lever. If you have axle nuts with washers, make sure they go on the outer face of each dropout (however, most axle nuts these days come as a single unit).

Look at the gap between the tyre and the top of the fork 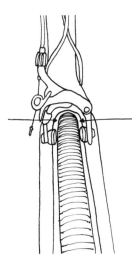 to ensure it is even on both sides, if it isn't, undo it, straighten it and do it up again.

CENTERED BETWEEN FRONT FORK

IMPORTANT: Always remember to re-attach your brakes! Give your wheel a spin to ensure the brakes are not rubbing.

REAR WHEEL

Slightly more complicated, but basically it's the same as taking it out only in reverse. Retract the rear derailleur, pulling it towards you to make space in the chain for the wheel to go in.

Guide the wheel between the brake blocks, and place the

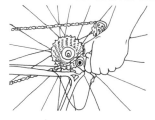

smallest sprocket of the rear cassette on the chain as you lower the axle into the dropouts.

Now, with your hands on either side of the axle, pull the wheel firmly all the way into the dropouts and do up the quick release or wheel nuts.

Make sure that the wheel is centered between the chain stays, if it is not, undo it, straighten it and redo it up again.

CENTRED BETWEEN CHAIN STAYS

NOTE: On a fixed gear bike the chain will need to be re-tensioned when replacing the rear wheel (see pp. 72-75).

Re-attach your brakes and give your wheel spin to ensure the brakes are not rubbing. Job done. Off you ride.

ALTERNATIVE PUNCTURE REPAIR

Sometimes fixing a puncture can be done on the fly. If you get a puncture and it's really obvious where it is - i.e. clear to see and/or hear, you may be able to mend the puncture without taking the wheel off.

Firstly, mark the tyre so you know where the hole is. If you have to move the bike in order to get away from traffic or for whatever other reason, do not push your bike - lift the wheel off the ground, so that the tyre doesn't move around the rim, making it difficult to locate the puncture.

Now lean your bike against a wall, and work with it in its normal upright position. Take your tyre levers and undo a section of the bead with the puncture as the central point - not a huge amount - just enough to extricate the damaged section of the inner tube.

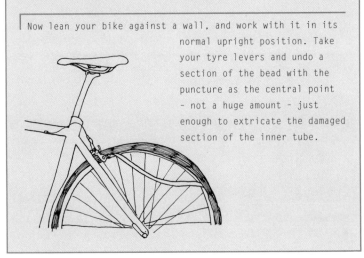

Remove whatever has done the damage and inspect the inside of the tyre to make sure there's no shard of horribleness left in there.

With the small section of inner tube exposed, pump it up slightly to check exactly where the hole is (you should have a pretty clear idea already). Now deflate the inner tube and repair it with your puncture repair kit (as per pp. 32-34), pop it back in, replace the section of exposed bead, pump it up and off you go. Bish bash bosh.

Brakes

Controlling your speed and stopping at short notice are pretty crucial when cycling, so it won't come as a huge surprise to hear that one of the key rules of bicycle safety is to make sure that your brakes are working properly.

Brakes vary from bike to bike, and before setting off on a new bike you should test the brakes to see how much force they require. For the most part, the front brake should take most of the heat when braking. The rule that generally applies is to put 75% of stopping power to the front brake and 25% to the rear. This has to do with transfer of weight to the front, preventing the rear wheel from skidding, and therefore wearing down quickly. Exceptions to this rule are braking when turning, on steep descents or when cycling on slippery surfaces. In these instances you should apply more pressure to the rear brake, as the front is more likely to skid, sending you head over handlebars.

It will be pretty clear when your brakes need urgent attention, but you should try to make sure it doesn't get to that point. Check them regularly: Squeeze the brake levers and push your weight down and forward on the handlebars. This should cause the rear of the bike to come up immediately. Do the same on the back brake, leaning your weight towards the rear wheel, causing the front wheel to come up. If the wheel rolls at all, or if you have to squeeze the brake levers all the way into your handlebars, you know it's time to get out your Allen key.

V-BRAKE

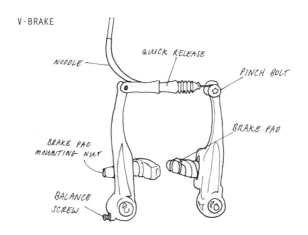

NOODLE

QUICK RELEASE

PINCH BOLT

BRAKE PAD

BRAKE PAD MOUNTING NUT

BALANCE SCREW

CALIPER BRAKE

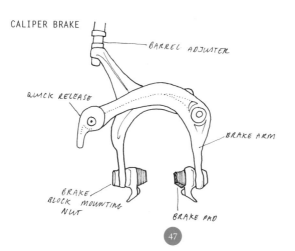

BARREL ADJUSTER

QUICK RELEASE

BRAKE ARM

BRAKE BLOCK MOUNTING NUT

BRAKE PAD

BARREL ADJUSTMENT

Over time your brake pads wear down, the cables may stretch, and you'll notice that the brakes are not working as effectively as they should. The easiest way to tighten them up is to use the 'barrel adjustment'.

On mountain bikes and hybrids with V-brakes you can find this on the brake lever. You'll see a lockring – undo this, and then simply turn the barrel adjuster counter-clockwise. Squeeze the brake levers, and when they feel tight enough, do the lockring back up.

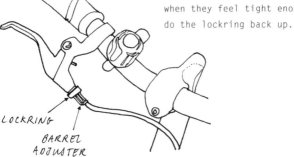

LOCKRING

BARREL
ADJUSTER

On most road bikes that use a caliper brake, you will find the barrel adjuster on the brakes themselves. On these there's no lockring - you just turn the barrel adjuster and check to see if the caliper arms are moving in or out. Squeeze the brake levers to check how tight they are.

BARREL
ADJUSTER

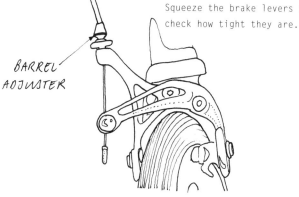

NOTE: Barrel adjustment is not an alternative to replacing worn brake pads. When the brake pads are really worn down, the barrel adjustment won't work. Also remember when you replace your brake pads, you will need to wind the adjustment all the way out to get the new pads in.

ADJUSTING THE BRAKE CABLE

There will come a time when the barrel adjuster has no more thread left to wind out, your brake levers are hitting the handlebars, and you just keep rolling. Not good. This is when you know your brake cable needs shortening.

CALIPER BRAKES

Start by winding the barrel adjuster all the way in, which will make the brake calipers come further apart

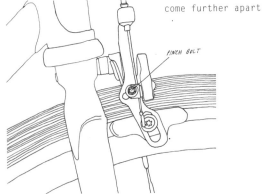

PINCH BOLT

Loosen the pinch bolt with the correct size Allen key,
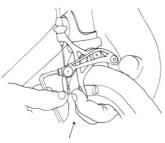 holding the cable at the
same time, so that the brake
calipers don't spring apart.
Once the pinch bolt is loose,
pull the brake blocks in tight
to the rim. With the blocks in
this position, pull some cable
through, making sure there is
no slack in the system.

HOLD PADS TOGETHER

Now tighten up the pinch bolt, securing the cable. Pump the
brake lever six or seven times to take any extra slack out.
You should really be able to feel the difference. If not,
repeat the process.

V-BRAKES

Undo the pinch bolt on the brake arm whilst holding the loose cable in one hand, so that the brake arms don't spring apart.

Pull some extra cable through. When the brake pad is almost touching the rim, retighten the pinch bolt, leaving a 2mm gap between pad and rim. Pump the brake six or seven times to take any slack out of the system. It should be much easier to brake. If not, you still have some slack so repeat the process.

You may find that after you've adjusted the cable, one brake

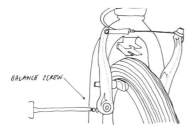

BALANCE SCREW

pad is sticking to the rim. If this happens, you'll need to centre the brakes so that the wheel spins freely. You'll notice that on the side of the brake arm towards the bottom there's a little screw - the balance screw. If you turn the balance screw clockwise, the brake pad will move away from the rim - anti-clockwise moves the pad in. Adjust the pad as you need to, squeezing the brake lever periodically to feel for the correct alignment. Now spin the wheel and check the space between the pads and the rim. Adjust both sides until the wheel spins freely.

BRAKE BLOCK REPLACEMENT

Most brake pads have a mark on them indicating when they need replacing. Keep an eye on this, and on the look and feel of the pads - apart from increasing your braking time, worn pads can damage the rim of your wheel, which is potentially both extremely dangerous and very expensive.

Replacing brake pads these days is much easier than it used to be. Most brake pads come in replaceable cartridges within the brake blocks, so all you have to do is remove your wheel, slip out the cartridge and slide the new one in. Shimano and Sram brakes usually have retaining screws that you can undo with a very small Allen key. Campagnolo brakes just slide out - but they are often a firm fit, and you may need the help of a pair of pliers to pull them out.

Remember, when re-inserting the brake pads that the opening

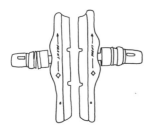

of the housing always faces towards the back and the sealed end towards the front. The pads or the housing will have an arrow marking forwards and another 'left and right' marking indicating which side they need to be fitted to.

There will be occasions, however, when you may need to remove the brake blocks entirely. It may be that they come in a sealed unit or that the replaceable cartridge just won't come out.

CALIPER BRAKE BLOCK REPLACEMENT

Start by undoing the brake block mounting nut. This is usually either a 5mm Allen key nut or a dome shaped nut, for which you will need a spanner. The pad and its housing should just slip off between the brake caliper and the rim when fully undone. Remove both brake blocks.

BRAKE BLOCK MOUNTING NUT

There are a number of washers either side of the brake arm. As each component comes off, lay it down in sequence, so that when you come to replace them the correct order is clear.

To fit your new brake pads, place the concave washer onto the brake pad housing and put the pad back on the caliper between the brake arm and the rim. Screw the nut with its washer to the outside of the caliper to secure the pad in place, but don't do it up too tight at this stage. Then put the opposite side on.

ANATOMY OF THE BRAKE BLOCK

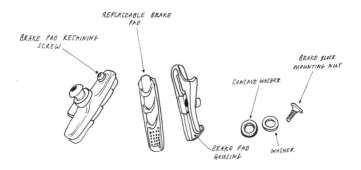

REPLACEABLE BRAKE PAD

BRAKE PAD RETAINING SCREW

BRAKE BLOCK MOUNTING NUT

CONCAVE WASHER

BRAKE PAD HOUSING

WASHER

Now to align the brakes. At this point you will need someone to hold the brake lever for you. If there's no kind soul readily available to perform this task, you can take an old toe-strap or some such thing to tie on and engage the brake while you are doing up and aligning the pads.

Once the brake lever is engaged, make sure the pad is

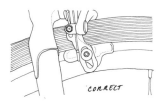

central to the braking surface and hits it square on. Some pads will be gently curved. These should follow the arch of the rim. At no point should your brake pads be touching the tyre.

CORRECT

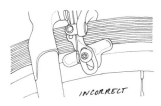

INCORRECT

Now the pad is in place, you can tighten the whole thing up. Hold the pad between your forefinger and thumb to stop it moving while you tighten. If it does move, just loosen it, reposition and tighten it again.

Release the brake lever and hey presto! You now have new pads.

V-BRAKE BLOCK REPLACEMENT

Firstly engage the brakes so that you can work with both hands. You can use the help of a friend to do this, or tie the brakes with some kind of strap.

Loosen the brake block mounting nut using a spanner or an Allen key. Remove all the components. On the outside of the brake arm, you'll find the brake block nut, the mounting washer, the concave washer and the convex washer.

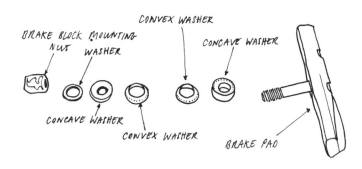

CONVEX WASHER

BRAKE BLOCK MOUNTING NUT WASHER

CONCAVE WASHER

CONCAVE WASHER

CONVEX WASHER

BRAKE PAD

Release the brake lever, and remove the components inside
the brake arm. You'll find a convex washer, concave washer
and the brake pad itself. Lay them out in order so you don't
get confused when it's time to put them back together.

TIP: If you do get confused, just remember that the convex
washers go on either side of the brake caliper, and the
concave washer fits over to form a ball - so you essentially
end up with a ball and socket joint. Alternatively, if you
remove one side at a time you'll have a point of reference.

Take your new brake block with its relevant washers and
pass the threaded bolt through the brake arm. Making sure
that the directional arrow is pointing forwards, align the
pad so that it is centred on the braking surface and the
curve of the pad follows the arch of the rim. At no point
should the pad touch the tyre or go below the rim.

Once the pad is in place, engage the brake lever again

(using your buddy or your strap), and put the outer washers on in the correct sequence. Then hold the brake pad firmly between your forefinger and thumb so that it doesn't move and tighten the outer nut.

TIP: If you've done all this only to find that there's not enough clearance between the pads and the rim for the wheel to run smoothly, do not despair. All you need to do is twist the barrel adjuster to allow the calipers to separate further. There should be about 1mm between the pad and the rim.

Gears

Adjusting gears is not for the faint-hearted. You have to really know your bike, and even then it can be a frustrating task to undertake. Trial and error is the only way to learn here. It is amazing to watch a bicycle mechanic in full flow adjusting the gears, switching them up and down constantly, listening and feeling for the moments when chain and sprocket do not engage properly and all the while chatting away, making it all look so simple. But the gears are the circulatory system of your bike, and without proper training, open-heart surgery is an operation you would do best to avoid.

Having said this, there are minor adjustments and problem solving that are definitely worth knowing. CPR if you will. Even these can be tricky to understand though, so hold on tight.

ADJUSTING GEARS

A bicycle mechanic will start you off by setting up your gears properly, but over time cables stretch, as does the chain, and the gears will not engage properly – skipping down or jumping off entirely when changing gears.

If this happens, there are three main adjustments that you can make on the rear derailleur, the barrel adjuster, (H) High limit screw, and the (L) Low limit screw.

ANATOMY OF THE REAR DERAILLEUR

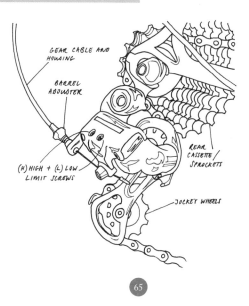

GEAR CABLE AND HOUSING

BARREL ADJUSTER

(H) HIGH + (L) LOW LIMIT SCREWS

REAR CASSETTE / SPROCKETS

JOCKEY WHEELS

BARREL ADJUSTER

The barrel adjuster is the first place to start when you
notice that your gears are not engaging properly. The
barrel adjuster alters the cable tension, allowing you to
fine tune your gears or re-adjust the indexing.

Change down to the highest gear, so that the chain is on
the smallest sprocket on the rear cassette and on the
largest sprocket on the front chainring.

With the rear wheel off the ground, turn the pedal so that
the chain and wheel are rotating. Now shift up one gear
with the front shifter. If you find that the chain does not
move or is letting out a clicking sound as it catches on
the sprocket above, change back down on the shifter.

TIP: This will be hard to do if you're on your own, so
ideally you'll get someone else to hold the rear wheel up
for you. Alternatively, you can do it while out riding:
Stop, make the adjustments, ride on a bit, and make further
adjustments. It's very stop-start, but effective.

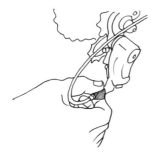

Rotate the barrel adjuster half a turn anti-clockwise to increase the tension on the cable, then move up a gear on the front shifter again and rotate the pedal to see if it shifts up smoothly. If it does, the tension is adequate. If you hear a rattle or a clicking sound, you may have twisted the barrel adjuster too far so that the chain is trying to advance to the next gear. In this instance, twist the barrel a quarter turn clockwise while still turning the pedal. If the clicking still doesn't stop, continue twisting in quarter increments clockwise until it does.

Now go through all the gears, advancing up by one, down two, to make sure that they're all working correctly. If it's slow and noisy advancing up, shift back down one and rotate the barrel adjuster anti-clockwise a quarter turn, then shift back up to see if that's fixed it. Apply the same principle to all the gears as you go through.

If you find that changing down gears is problematic, the cable is too tight. Rotate the barrel adjuster clockwise a quarter turn each time until it evens out.

To summarise:
If you have problems shifting up gears, your cable is too loose and you need to tighten it by turning the barrel adjuster anti-clockwise. If the shift is slow or does not go down, the cable is too tight and you need to loosen it by turning the barrel adjuster clockwise.

If, after endless tinkering, you find that you are able to change up smoothly but not down - or the other way round - it could be that your cable needs replacing. Get a mechanic to do this for you.

NOTE: When the chain is on the largest rear sprocket and the largest front sprocket, or alternatively on the smallest rear sprocket and smallest front sprocket, you will almost always hear a scraping noise or a slight rattle. This is because the chain is at its maximum limit and this gear should not be used that often. As long as your gears are shifting smoothly between all the others, this is nothing to worry about.

(H) HIGH LIMIT SCREW

If your gears are set up correctly, when the chain is on
the smallest sprocket at the back and biggest sprocket at
the front, the highest gear, the jockey wheels will be
sitting directly under the smallest sprocket perfectly in
line when viewed from behind the bike. If this is not the
case and it is out line, it may cause your chain to jump
off towards the chain stays, and you will need to adjust
the (H) High limit screw.

In the highest gear, slacken off the (H) limit screw until

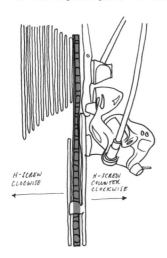

H-SCREW
CLOCKWISE

H-SCREW
COUNTER
CLOCKWISE

there is no resistance. Now
turn the (H) limit screw
clockwise to bring the jockey
wheels directly in line under
the smallest sprocket when
viewed from behind the bike.
Rotating the screw clockwise
moves the jockey wheel to the
left and rotating the screw
anti-clockwise will move it
to the right. When you turn
the pedal the chain should be
running smooth. If there is a
slight clicking sound, turn the
(H) limit screw very slightly
- half turns at a time - to the
left or right, until it stops.

(L) LOW LIMIT SCREW

This is the same procedure as before but with the chain on the biggest sprocket at the back and the smallest sprocket on the front - the lowest gear. The jockey wheels should be directly in line with largest sprocket if you're looking at it from behind the bike.

Loosen the (L) limit screw until there is no resistance.

You will notice that the cage for the jockey wheels is sitting very close to the spokes of the wheel. Now retighten the (L) limit screw so that the jockey wheels sit directly under the largest sprocket, vertically in line with each other when viewed from behind.

L-SCREW COUNTER CLOCKWISE

L-SCREW CLOCKWISE

One of the beauties of riding fixed/single speed is its pure
simplicity; you and your machine working as one. With no
gears to contend with, your legs regulate the change in
pace - pedal faster you go faster. On a fixed gear you are
literally plugged into your machine, developing a closer
relationship with bike and road.

All this considered, the chain will need to be tensioned
occasionally as it becomes slack over time.

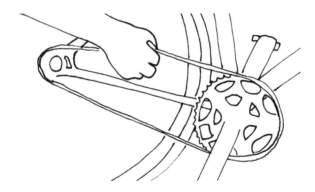

To tighten up the chain, undo the wheel nut on the neutral side (opposite side to the chain) and pull the wheel over slightly to the neutral side. Then tighten up the wheel nut.

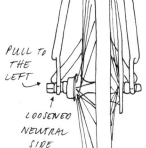

PULL TO
THE
LEFT

↑
LOOSENED
NEUTRAL
SIDE

You will notice that the wheel is slightly off-centre between the chain stays. Loosen the drive side wheel nut, push the wheel back slightly towards the drive side, and retighten the wheel nut on that side.

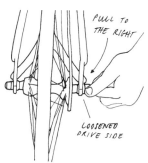

PULL TO
THE RIGHT

LOOSENED
DRIVE SIDE

What you are effectively doing is walking the wheel back in the dropout from left to right, increasing the chain tension as you go. Each time you pull the wheel over to one side, check the tension on the chain – you don't want it too tight or you will just wear it out quicker. The chain on a fixed wheel bike should only be able to move a total of 20-25mm up and down, i.e. 10-12mm up and 10-12mm down from the centre. Any more than this and it needs adjusting and less it is obviously too tight.

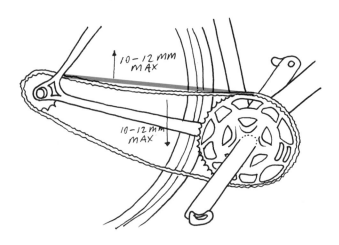

Once you have enough tension on the chain, check to ensure the wheel is centered between the chain stays, if it isn't, loosen the neutral side wheel nut and centre it. Finally, double check that your wheel nuts are securely done up and hey presto, you're off.

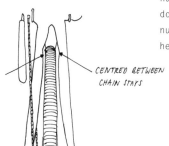

CENTRED BETWEEN
CHAIN STAYS

When you feel you have the correct tension in the chain, take the pedal through a full revolution and watch the tension on the chain as it goes round. You'll see that there are tighter and looser spots. You need to find a happy medium, making sure the tight spots are not too tight or the loose spots too loose. Watch your fingers!

Maintenance

In the same way that personal hygiene keeps bugs at bay, keeping your bike reasonably presentable will give you a much more trouble free as well as a better looking ride. It's really important to know the basics of maintenance on your bike – to make sure all the parts are clean and operating correctly. It will make the bike run better, reduce wear and tear, and will keep you in synch with your bike, aware of its parts and its condition at any given moment.

How much maintenance is required differs according to usage. However, all bikes deserve a little bit of regular loving – a clean and a good old lube once every two or three months and additional basic tests every month or so. Don't neglect it. Don't let it get mangy and sad. Keep it happy and it will make you happy.

2. HEADSET / BRAKES

1. FRONT WHEEL

4. SEAT TUBE/
SADDLE

5. REAR
WHEEL/
DERAILLEUR

TTOM BRACKET/
CHAIN

Once a month, it's worth giving your bike a proper once over, to make sure that it's roadworthy. The M-check follows the shape of the bike frame, assessing the condition of each of its components, and should take five minutes or so. It's also a good idea to do an M-check if you're buying a second-hand bike – any nasty defects will quickly become apparent.

STEP 1: FRONT WHEEL

QUICK RELEASE LEVERS/WHEEL NUTS

Open your quick release levers and then close them. They

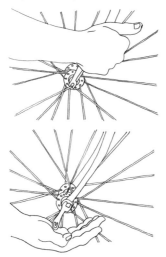

should be tight enough that it requires a fair bit of force to close them. If you have wheel nuts, use a spanner to ensure they are tightened properly.

BEARINGS

The hub of the wheel has ball bearings inside that can

sometimes get loose or worn down. With the bike parallel to you, get hold of the wheel and the top of the fork blade and move the wheel backwards and forwards to see if there is any movement in the hub. If there is, you will need to have this looked at by a professional.

WHEEL RIM AND SPOKES

Look for excessive wear on the rim of the wheel. The braking surface should be flat. If it's concave or has hairline cracks, this means your wheel has worn out and needs replacing.

Run your hand over the spokes, making sure none of the spokes are loose, broken or even missing - if they are, they need to be repaired straight away by a professional.

Give your wheel a spin and look at the gap between the wheel and the brake blocks, to make sure it is true. It will probably have a slight wobble - but you want the gap to be relatively consistent and not growing and shrinking as the wheel revolves. If it's more than 1mm either way, this will need to be looked at by a professional.

TYRES

Give your tyre a good squeeze to test the pressure, it shouldn't have much give. If it does you need to pump it up to the right pressure (PSI), which should be indicated on your tyre wall (see p. 21).

Check the surface of your tyre for any holes or cuts, stones or pieces of glass that may need to be picked out.

Look for any signs of cracking or bulges in the tyre - indications that your tyre is worn out and needs to be replaced.

STEP 2: HEADSET AND BRAKES

BRAKES

Make sure that your brake pads are not worn out. In most cases, there will be an indicator line that will tell you if they are. If so replace them (see pp. 54-60).

Check that the brake blocks are aligned properly. Apply the brakes and make sure the blocks are hitting the rim squarely and at no point touch the tyre.

Apply both the brake levers, pushing your weight down and forward on the handlebars, causing the rear of the bike to come up. Do the same with the back brake, causing the front to come up. If the wheel slips though the blocks, they need to be adjusted (see pp. 48-52).

HANDLEBARS AND HEADSET

Holding the front wheel between your legs, twist the handlebars both up and down and side to side to ensure they are tight. Give your brake levers a good wiggle to check they are secure.

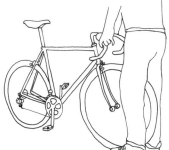

Still with the front wheel between your legs, apply the front brake and push backwards and forwards to see if there is any play or movement in the headset. If there is, you'll need to have this tightened.

Look at the handlebar stem to ensure it is inserted correctly. On some stems there is a max height and min insert mark - make sure it's in between the two. This also applies to the seat post.

STEP 3: BOTTOM BRACKET AND CHAIN

The bottom bracket is the heart of your bicycle. It's what keeps your bike rigid and therefore strong. Positioning yourself on one side of the bike, hold the seat tube in one hand and with the other, turn the crank arm to 12 o'clock and move it towards and away from the seat tube to see if there is any play or movement. Rotate the crank to 6 o'clock then pass your arm through the frame and move the opposing pedal forwards and back to see if there is any play on this side. If you encounter any movement in either crank you will need to get this looked at.

CHAIN

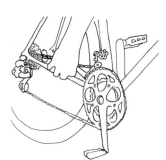

While you are down here have a good look at the chain. Turn the pedal backwards, feeling and listening to the chain. Is it running free? Perform a visual check, if your chain is a reddy brown then it is rusty and needs lubricating. Feel it with your fingers, is there too much oil? Is there too much slack in the chain? If so, your chain will need tightening.

STEP 4: SEAT TUBE / SADDLE

Grab hold of the saddle and try to lift it by the nose and twist it through its length to ensure it is secure.

STEP 5: BACK WHEEL

Follow the same sequence as the front wheel, checking your quick release levers/wheel nuts, bearings and spokes and spin the wheel to see how true it is. Check the tyre and the braking surface of the wheel rim, as well as the brake pads.

Give your gears a once over, running through them to ensure they change properly.

Inspect the rear mechanism, making sure it is fastened

 well and there are no teeth missing or damage/excessive wear on the rear cassette and jockey wheels.

FRAME

During the whole process of the M-check always scrutinise
your frame looking for any damage, wear or cracks.

The full M-check needs to be done monthly, but every time
you ride, give a quick glance to the ABC of roadworthiness:

AIR: CHECK YOUR
TYRES ARE THE
CORRECT PRESSURE.

BRAKES: APPLY
THEM AND ENSURE
THEY WORK CORRECTLY

CHAIN: MAKE SURE
IT IS PROPERLY
LUBRICATED.

CLEANING

Cleaning your bike can be a very satisfying experience, as well as a valuable one. Dirty bikes are just less pleasant to ride – the chain will wear down quicker and the gears will be slow to shift. A proper 25-minute clean will keep it running smooth and looking sharp.

How often you clean your bike depends on how you're riding it. If you're an off-road cyclist churning it up in wet, muddy conditions, you should give it a clean every time you ride. If you're an average commuter cyclist, a thorough clean once every three months or so will suffice with regular wipe-downs and chain-lubes in between.

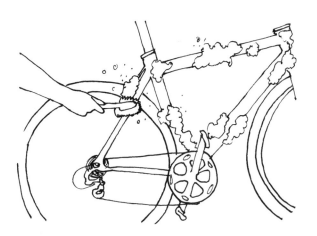

Fill a bucket with hot water mixed with a bit of washing up liquid. You can get bike-specific cleaning products, but they're not essential. Take a long-handled washing up brush and scrub the whole frame, getting into all the nooks and crannies of the wheels, rear derailleur, front mech and chain. Use a couple different scrubbers or sponges, so you avoid getting grease on the saddle and handlebars.

Once your bike is looking pretty clean, fill your bucket

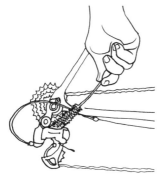

with clean hot water and sponge off the excess soap. You'll notice that around the rear mech and the front chain ring, the water is beading and the black grime has not shifted. For this you will need a degreaser. I prefer citrus degreasers, as they're kinder to the environment and don't give you a headache. Dip your smaller scrubbing brush or toothbrush into the degreaser and scrub the rear cassette, chain, derailleur, front chainrings and anywhere else with an accumulation of grease.

TIP: I'm very particular about my rags. Old cotton towels or sheets are best. I avoid synthetic fibres like the plague – they just aren't absorbent enough and occasionally dissolve in solvents.

Once all the old grease has been dissolved, you need to rinse it off thoroughly with hot water. If it was really greasy and the residue is not coming off with hot water alone, use hot soapy water first and then rinse it again with clean hot water.

TIP: Avoid using a high pressure hose when washing off your bike. Forcing water into the sensitive bearings of the bottom bracket, headset and hubs can cause all sorts of problems.

Dry your bike off with a clean cloth or chamois, getting

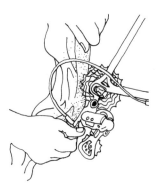

into all the tight spots. You will need to clean out the rear cassette and remove any water that is still in there. You could give it a squirt of GT85 or WD40 before you do this. Hold the rag taut in your hands and run the edge between each of the gear sprockets. As you pull down, the ratchet will rotate towards you, so by moving the rag up and down, you'll be able to reach in between each of the gears.

To dry and clean the chain, get a clean rag and hold
it around the chain. Then rotate the pedal backwards,
applying enough pressure to the rag so that the chain can
pass through, thus removing all the excess water and any
remaining dirt. It's also worth wiping the teeth of the
front chainring. Rotate the pedal, exposing the teeth all
the way around as you wipe.

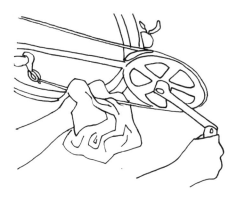

Your bike should be looking great by now, but your job is
not over yet.... Time to get out that lube....

LUBRICATION

Lubrication is essential to the smooth running of your bike. It protects your bike from the wear caused by the friction of components against one another and prevents the metal elements from rusting. How often you lube and what you use depends on riding conditions. In normal circumstances once a month will probably suffice, using a dry lube that attracts little dirt. If you are constantly riding in wet and muddy conditions, you will need to lube after every ride, and to use a wet lube – which is heavier and sticks to the chain better.

The art of lubrication is more delicate than you would expect. Too little lubrication and the components will freeze up and rust, too much and they will attract dirt, forming an abrasive paste that will wear down your components.

CHAIN

Make sure your chain is clean before you apply new

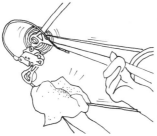

lubricant. If it is really filthy and needs a degreaser, the whole bike probably needs cleaning. Otherwise, just get a clean rag, make a pad and hold it around the chain, spinning the pedal so that the chain passes through the rag, removing the old grease and dirt.

Take the rag and hold it taut between each of the rear sprockets, moving it up and down like flossing. Wipe the front teeth of the chainring.

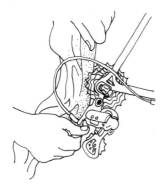

Once the chain is clean it's time to lube up. Lay a rag

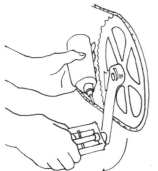

directly under the chain to catch any drips, and apply the lubricant to the upper surface of the lower part of the chain - the section of the chain below the chain stays and between the front ring and the rear derailleur.

Turn the pedal backwards while you dribble oil on every single link. When the whole chain has been covered, take a clean rag, hold it around the chain and rotate the chain through the rag to remove any excess oil. The chain wants to be almost dry to the touch, just slightly tacky between your fingers.

CABLES

To lubricate your cables, use a product like GT85 or WD40

with a nozzle attachment. The general method of application is to spray it gently into the housing of the individual cables.

Start with the brake cables. Pull your brake levers in. You should be able to see the start of the brake cable underneath. Spray in here. Then go to the brake caliper and spray the point at which the cable comes out of the housing.

BRAKE CALIPER →

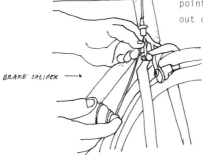

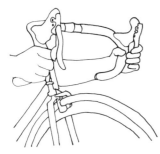

Next squirt some lube on the point where the cable comes out along the top tube.
Finally, go back to the brake lever and pump it a few times to work the lubricant along the brake cable towards the centre.

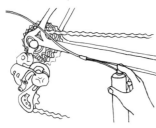

A similar procedure follows for the gear cables: go to the shifters and spray the point where the gear cables come in. Then spray the points in the front and rear derailleur where the cable is exposed. Finally, work the cables by shifting the gears up and down several times so that the lubricants work along the cables.

When applying the spray lubricant, take extra care not to get any on the rims or braking surfaces and always wipe off any excess.

REPLACING THE PEDALS

On occasion you may need to remove your pedals – they might need replacing, or you may be traveling with your bike.

Pedal threads are different on both sides. The left hand side has a left hand thread, so is undone clockwise and goes on anti-clockwise. The right hand side has a right hand thread, so is undone anti-clockwise and goes on clockwise. The pedals will be marked respectively with a (L) and (R). You may notice that the (L) one has striations and the (R) one is smooth at the spindle.

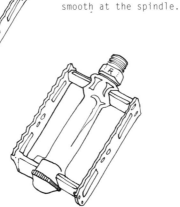

REMOVING

You'll need a pedal spanner for this job. Fit the spanner

onto the two flat edges of the pedal spindle. The spanner should not be in front of the pedal, but rather running parallel to the crank arm at a 90 degree angle or less.

Turn the pedal spanner either clockwise or anti-clockwise

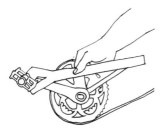

depending on what side you are removing. If you hold the opposite crank arm, you can rotate it as if pedaling forward. You will have to experiment with different positions to get the right leverage.

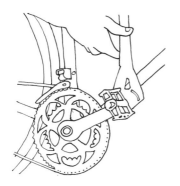

INSTALLING

It is good practice to apply grease to the thread of the pedals before you screw them in. Locate the marks on the pedals telling you which side it goes on and screw the pedals on by hand to begin with. Rotate the crank arm backwards as you are screwing them up - you will find that they go on quicker. Once they're finger tight, get your pedal spanner and tighten them up. Some pedals will require an Allen key to tighten them up. Note that in this instance your multi-tool won't give you the leverage you need - you'll need a long 6mm or 8mm Allen key to do the job.

Pedals installed!

TIP: Put the chain onto the largest chainring at the front - this will save your knuckles if you slip with spanner.

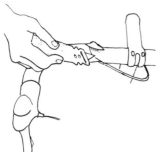

This is a very satisfying task, one that rewards your patience and scrutiny. A good wrap is something to be proud of, especially if you have forked out a huge sum of money for leather bar tape.

Start by removing any tape that may already be on the bars using a Stanley knife or a pair of scissors. You don't want to cut any of the cable housing, or if you have carbon bars, you don't want to be scoring them, so do this carefully.

With all the old bar tape off, unravel the new tape and

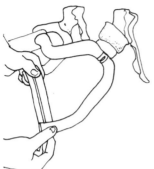

start the roll at the bottom of the bar. Don't start it flush with the end. You want to leave an overhang here, which will eventually be stuffed into the bar-end opening, and sealed with a bar plug when the wrapping is completed.

Begin winding the tape around the bar, overlapping as you

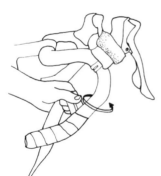

go. There's nothing worse than loose bar tape, so hold the tape taut while wrapping it around, but not so tight that the tape tears. Try to keep the overlap sections even, and make sure there are no gaps between the wraps. You may need to keep working the tape - pulling it and backing it up to get it right. Take your time on the corners - it has to look good after all.

Your pack of bar tape will have come with an extra piece

of tape. When you get to your brake levers, place that extra piece at the back of the shifter that connects the brake to the handlebar.

Now lift the brake hood and pull the tape up along the

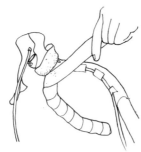

inside edge of the brake and back around onto the top section of the handlebar. Wind it around a few times and then go back and pull the brake hood cover back down to ensure that the area around the brake is covered with no gaps.

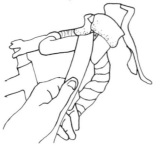

Continue winding the tape along the top section of the bars

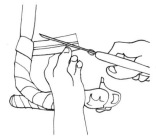

until you reach the end. Take a sharp knife and score the tape along the ending line. Now unravel the tape a couple of turns and cut along the scored line, which should be at an angle. Wrap this tapered end back around the bar to make a neat end.

Use some black electrical tape, usually supplied in your

pack, to secure the bar tape to the bar neatly.

Finally, poke the surplus tape that you let hang over end

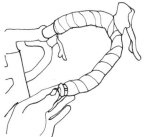

at the start into the end of the bar and place the bar end plug in to secure it and finish it all off.

CCH

For extra tips, look for us on
www.thebikeownershandbook.com,
www.tboh.tumblr.com, twitter
and facebook.

Many thanks to all the people who
helped make this book happen.
Thanks to Ziggy Hanaor at Cicada
Books for being an all round
superstar. To our talented and
mega-speedy illustrator Phil Smith.
To Lisa at April for our funky
layouts. To Graeme Fife for his lovely
foreword. To Jules at Cyclefit and Joe
at Rapha for their general input and
advice, and a special thanks to all at
Look Mum No Hands, a fantastic
bike shop and café in Old Street,
London. Managers Matt, Lewin
and Sam, who gave us technical
advice, amazing coffee and let us use
their workshop facilities. Digger, a
mechanical maestro, starred
in our video clips and entertained
us with a constant stream of witty
banter that made the process that
much more enjoyable.

Published by Cicada Books Limited

Written by Peter Drinkell
Foreword by Graeme Fife
Photography and video links by Peter Drinkell
Illustrations by Phil Smith
(www.philsmithart.tumblr.com)
Edited by Ziggy Hanaor
Designed by Joana Niemeyer and Lisa Sjukur
for April (www.studio-april.com)

British Library Cataloguing-in-Publication Data

A CIP record for this book is available from
the British Library.
ISBN: 978-0-9562053-8-4

© 2012 Cicada Books Limited

look mum no hands!

www.lookmumnohands.com

AUG 17 2012

CO

Cicada Books Limited
85 Parkhill Road
London NW3 2XY

T: +44 207 267 5208
E: ziggy@cicadabooks.co.uk
W: www.cicadabooks.co.uk